Year *of the* Labyrinth

CMUP Poetry

Jake Grefenstette, Series Editor

Also by Brian Sneeden

Poetry

Last City

Translation

Homerica

Cicada

Chimera

Goatsong

Year *of the* Labyrinth

Brian Sneeden

Carnegie Mellon University Press
Pittsburgh 2026

Acknowledgments

Grateful acknowledgment is made to the following publications in which some of these poems first appeared:

Academy of American Poets' Poem-a-Day: "Memory Is Blood Soluble"
Amsterdam Review: "Tomatoes"
Gulf Coast: "Cloudberries"
Gutter: "Your Bandura"
Indiana Review: "Other Fountains"
Iowa Review: "Origins," "Season of Echoes"
Matter: "Year of the Labyrinth"
Montreal Poetry Prize Anthology: "Darkness Passional"
Poetry: "Chimeras"
Poetry Review: "Instructions for the Cure"
Poetry Ireland Review: "We Didn't Have a Proper Witch," "What We Did When We Were Ghosts"
Puerto Del Sol: "Fissure," "Meli," "Must There Be No Invisible World"
Southern Review: "Dear Shipwreck," "Found Poems in Translation," "Snow Wine"
Western Humanities Review: "Laurels"

"Origins" and "Season of Echoes" were awarded the *Iowa Review* Award for Poetry. "Cloudberries" was awarded the *Gulf Coast* Barthelme Prize. "Other Fountains" was awarded the *Indiana Review* 1/2K Prize. "Darkness Passional" was shortlisted for the Montreal Poetry Prize and the Janet B. McCabe Poetry Prize.

"Darkness Passional," "Fissure," "Memory is Blood Soluble," appeared in Arabic translation in the magazine *Al-Arabi*, translated by Anas Tarif; "Must There Be No Invisible World" and "We Didn't Have a Proper Witch" appeared in Serbian translation in *Eckermann*, translated by Danijela Trajković.

Book design by Connie Amoroso

Library of Congress Control Number 2026937113
ISBN 978-0-88748-744-6
Copyright © 2026 by Brian Sneeden
All rights reserved
Printed and bound in the United States of America

10 9 8 7 6 5 4 3 2 1

Contents

III.

"Elsewhere is a negative mirror."

—*Italo Calvino* (*tr. William Weaver*)

Season of Echoes

I came to a mirror in the road and passed through it, painlessly. Almost without noticing. A change of wind. Nothing rustled. I peeled a leaf from the air. Then everything started again, and I walked forward, back to the village. All of it was the same, down to the last detail, except that somewhere a window was missing or a bird that hadn't yet been invented began to sing. In the root-spurt, strands of verbena stuck to wet clay, a blackbird picked fleece from a nude patch of field. Days passed, and I couldn't sleep for wondering which was the reflected world.

I

Origins

At the pollen line
where the belly of the coyote drags
its chain of meat

in tick-smeared grass,
snout wet
from throat, fur

I slick with my tongue
as rehearsal for eating
what I love. There is no place

but mouth
for opening the animal
by the curve

of its name.
In a worry of jacarandas
a deer shape

bleeds into the field
with its cage
of self

and self-sensing,
watches from the other side
of reeds that border

sleep that borders
what I cannot allow,
its eyes hovering in field

I carry always like an amulet,
like a branch simultaneously
burned

and burning, the smell
of ozone
and chrysanthemums. The ember

that passed through my voice
seeded cities—ellipses
and salt.

Cloudberries

In August your father goes up the mountain in a bark suit with bear claws to harvest cloudberries. This is the season of rain and buried sunlight. When he comes home you're stuck inside for two days with the windows sealed to keep out wasps, boiling juice in the vat, poking the pulp into jars. Afterwards, the smell of cooling metal and your father smoking. Of the planets in the evening as the steam disperses his is darkest. One day you find his bark suit hanging in the attic and put it on, swaying your claws like a bear in the aubergine patch. When it happens you see nothing but a drip and think you manifested berries in the air. That it was your gift. Later, changing rags over your brother's missing eye, he describes the unbearable pain of seeing without dimension. You imagine your punishments: changed into a bear and chased by your own dogs, locked in a tower with nothing to eat but soup made from your hair, your arm sewn into a beehive and stung a thousand times a day for a hundred and one days. When your father comes home your brother says: *the bear got away.* Winter came. The season of brine and black bread. All day it sleeps in the attic, its peeling barkflesh fuzzed with burrs. Any bird would avoid it. In the mornings you leave out a bowl of melted snow, and at night can sometimes hear the awkward graze of claws.

Darkness Passional

Is each turn in the ground
a mystery? What I grow reaffirms
an old trick, humus plus longing,
a formula for living in isolation

without resistance. Without forgiveness,
or praying for the body to open
at any other than its own speed.
Who else will winter in the eye

of a crow? This bedding of rods
and stems, and absolution like a body
of water I do not know the name of,
or the name I wore when I sank

to the bottom, the arcs of my fingers
a chalk smear darkening in pulses.
Who else enters when I'm on my way
to the other body, a vision of rice field

and black water and cloud-curious
lightning. Transmigratory. I don't mean legumes
or the way Pythagoras imagined the soul
folded upon itself like a library

in the umbilical protein of a bean's
wrinkly bit. I already know we are edible
and whisper to each other while eating
the ones we did not name. I mean

this repeating field where the role play
of prey and hunter ad nauseams. How many times
was I the deer, my recurring volta
through undergrowth and mulch

continuing even now on someone's screen.
If memory is just rented from the humus, then
when it's my turn in the ground
go bury me in an acre of wind.

Snow Wine

To sanitize the vineyard we halve a pomegranate with a paring knife & walk in circles flicking seeds. In the *Papyri Graecae Magicae* a white rooster is preferred, gripped firmly at the feet & ripped down the middle by two women walking opposite paths. It seems essential the blood curve symmetrically. The biochemist says: blood is acidic, like vines, simple soil amendment. But a decanted rooster fills maybe two glasses. Only ritual does this. The priestesses wore white, from a distance resembling snow or elision, trailing blood in wind-dust & thirst, until two halves meet & the bird is buried whole. Barely ripe, the pomegranate stains our fingers prying out each humane seed. When we reach the middle we eat the last then lay the joined halves like a deflated ball in the scrub. Avoid improvisation, no god said. Because: how to acquire the eye of a man who died watching hyacinths? Or a hanged godmother's talus? We substitute tea of powdered eyebright & flowering goosefoot. In this way we avoid pesticides, chemical fertilizers, late blight, early frost, neighbors, strays. In June, thunder gifts us new rabbits. By August the grapes flicker like sleeping eyelids & later we'll harvest them delicately with hands braceleted in wasps. How to officiate two acres of future seabed? The source text falters. Inside its missing fragments, static furls like within a seashell. You say: place a cicada on your tongue & wait.

We Didn't Have a Proper Witch

But Gran Bradie who'd tool with potatoes
for curing warts, take her pin and open the eye

of a red Norland and rub it gainst any cultivar
of blemish (dog-pip, filiform) and plant it

in her yarden wrapped in white cloth. And when
the tubers swole it slivered on the edge like

an oxidized coin filed to wrinkles. What she did
with the spuds after I don't know. There are

gardeners in it for the thinning and dead-
heading, lancing foliage the body leaves. Probably

she hashed them with the skins on and fried
with duck eggs. Like when the clergy of Antioch

drove white cattle through the street, their throats
hidden in the static of eucalyptus and doublemint

for sacrifice, everyone else lined the road lifting
amphora for leftovers. Given a chance, steal

your spot of scried meat from the worm's mouth.
Maybe she smothered them with dirt, returning

earth to earth. All I know is once I had one
then I didn't. Maybe someone ate the spud.

Laurels

In the story the god chases her
into a field, his shadow changing
from wolf, to leopard, to man,

and she is forced to use up
her one good spell
to turn into a hare, a gazelle, a tree.

The god is the victim.
He sings: silence is the wheat
of heartache, etc.

Then he waits till no one is around
and quietly steals her branches.
In the story she bends

into the part of herself
that's empty field
with moonlight. In the story

she's a door in the hillside—
when she opens
she vanishes.

Mother Tongue

Inside her
        you're drinking eclipse water
laced with mint.
It's the season of broken
        chrysanthemums & all night a river
hums algae
from the bodying threads
        of your breath.
By mother tongue
they mean what you'll say
        with her milk in your teeth. Your
first articulated thirsts,
moon tugged
        in the mouth. Sometimes *river*
will feel like falling
asleep in her hair & waking up
        in a boat you don't know how to steer:
there are reefs & random
outcroppings. It's
        believed you arrive somewhere
on this mother &
mothered tongue. Soon
        in the field next door
an animal will slick & land
in hay, the yolk of

        her first body clinging
as she stands, shaking
from the floor, the ordinary bone
        & ligaments glittering
with breath.

Fire Pruning

A flame carries fire's memory. How else would it know what to do? The memorized notes of cathedral plinths and dried herbs. The peat hints and dark undermeats of fir roots. In the article I translate for practice a man in Thessaloniki describes returning to his orchard after, pruning the black and sap-stained scaffolds, burning his hand on a swollen graft with the word *enargeia*: bright unbearability. We never had the choice to be inedible. But can it recognize in the charred resins the terroir of Roman triremes: creosote, harbor rope. Or a filter on the still burning cigarette stolen from the lips of a corpse at the docks. I don't know if fire purifies the way we think, or just transfers baggage to an awaiting life. Ask flame and it'll say: don't mind brightness. Maybe ruin pollinates. Time grows fertile. Maybe he sits above the city with his secateurs, delicately thinning the smoke.

Apollo Boy

My son, let's promise
never to grow walls from
our blood. It's no longer late

in the world, or so I read
in the hyacinths
from the meadow where the discus lands

off-screen, in the Greek
tradition. Let's pretend
it is early, and the synonyms

for home still hesitate
between shelter and sky,
and we have one word

for stranger and nearest
friend. The sun rises and
sets in the same consonant.

But in this translation you
are the son, and I am
the one returning

the burn of embers, the snakebite,
the spinning disc that ruptures
speech. In the same world

where everything waits
to wound you to cherish you
let's promise no walls.

Memory Is Blood Soluble

I am still the old man with the street organ and cat, turning the same crank and expecting moonlight. What I remember: smoke of houses on the riverbank. Storm on mute. Temple broken, lamb-entered. You loved my bones because they were white. In the gathering blindness, you bandaged my body, and in doing so made it my body. I can't remember which chord heals visions or causes them. Which summons a cloud of bees from the stone or conceals your shape behind a flame. It is every guitar I have found in the gutter. Every name on the edge of being gone.

Choras

1.

A cat's protection is a clean curse.
In exchange for

nearness, crumbs
you hadn't realized you left

in the bed, the bookcase. The edible
shadow of your longest grief.

One cat can do much with
even this. Even

the thoughtless drift at night
of a hand to comfort emptiness.

2.

In the village across lights are waiting to turn on.
Waiting for the cat to finish batting the dead briefcase,

to close once and for all its hidden eye and begin
the streetlights with a stab of its tail. Waiting for the black fin

of the kitos (choose: whale or sea monster).
Waiting for the woman braiding her daughter's hair

with a thread that is her secret memory of orange blossoms
returning every March like the orbit of her humming wrists.

After, she raises a mirror for her daughter to see
the light of two villages, and a cat licking its tail.

II

Year of the Labyrinth

It was October and the tourists who barricaded the port had boarded their ferries and aeroplanes and like climbing down a blue door in the sea, were gone. The ghosts returned from the mountain in pairs, holding torches you could see from the plaza like headlights. The baited lines of the fishermen pulled up fenders and bicycles with the wheels still spinning. I go for a walk beneath the still-working streetlight of Odos Lithos. It is contagious as language, this repeating village, where the dripping of the octopus limb on the table, the swallowed coin of the child, the fallen apple quickened to static in the whirred room of the wasp return to their originals. Had it not always been there, translated in our sleep, I would not know which came first: the labyrinth or the entrails of the lamb.

Other Orchards

Each year the same village grows on the mountain.
A spiral polyp of balconies where everything
resembles itself but wrong: stairwells ascending

into ceilings, airless chimneys. Yesterday a shepherdess
living alone in the valley ignored it; today, a fisherman
tying his net with his teeth. No one came

though a road gradually curled to its innermost street.
Children gathering corals in the green shallows beneath
the cliff sing: *voiceless city / Petro picked / from*

your windows, your doors / empty apples / now
he's turned into / a cicada / lonely grove / apple me
no more. Who's Petro? Maybe he's me. A stray or sacrifice.

One who wakes inside an existing life and does
the honest thing: acquire his breath. Because labyrinth
without loss isn't. And I have nowhere to be.

Must There Be No Invisible World

In the village one night there was a dream that was contagious. A woman stood inside the fountain speaking an impossible language as neighbours drifted like recent ghosts after an earthquake. In the morning a strange taste, like ozone and rosewater. Now a staircase grows in the centre of the fountain in the square. No one remembers when it started. One night, two boys sneak from their rooms and climb down the steps, careful not to get their shoes wet. If one asks in this village about the children or the staircase, they will tell you what the price of fish will be when market opens, on what side of the cypress moss was growing. And now and again, in the folds of a zucchini flower or the placenta of a tomato one finds a drenched shoelace, a scalp of thread.

Tomatoes

The morning I split my tooth you crossed an acre of red concrete cupping a tomato plant in your palm. It was the week before thrushes and after robins, when the rain is suddenly warm. We planted it in the gutter beneath our kitchen window and it grew embarrassingly full on our neglect, a few eroded leaves and runoff. By August we fed daily, each one indigo with yellow cracks, the skins thick and musical. At first the symptoms were playful: you dreamt of shipwrecks and your acupuncturist gave you wet herbs in a glass. One night I woke up playing *L'isle joyeuse* on the out of tune piano. In the night shade we visited each other's dreams and read letters by the light of our skin. When your results come back with elevated lead we buy a kit and test everything: the knobs and faucets, the chipping paint on the mirror, the gryphon's toes of the clawfoot tub. Then a strip lands on the cutting board and purples: positive. That night I opened a tomato and felt a tooth. We pulled it up by the roots and buried it in a field beneath the beams of our headlights. For weeks afterwards we swallowed gigantic pills and drank lemon water. Then one morning I woke and you were nowhere. I searched all day but couldn't find you, though you were reading on the couch, though you were brushing your teeth over the sink. We asked: which one of us is the ghost? You left and went to live with a friend. I stayed. In spring I look out the kitchen window and see the new crop seeded in the clogged gutter, the blameless white florets I can't bring myself to cut.

Meli

Where there is honey for sale by the road which is like honeys sold in plywood stands by other roads on the island, except here it grows from the stones of old statues submerged in seawater. After a few months, long indigo fibers sprout from the rocks and are cut into the shapes of bees and hung inside boxes. At night you can see them lit up, like purple lanterns on the mountain. If the first night is a full moon, it is said their honey will heal arthritis, dry mouth, eczema, memories, snakebites, fallen arches, shrapnel, whispers, journeys—a rare condition of hearing goat bells in a tunnel. If the first night is any other night, the honey will only be honey, but a dark indigo kind that glows in the cupboard and on the tongue, and on the body of the one you love when you smear it on his ankles and on his throat and will, from time to time, sting.

Memento Mori

Our secrets are bird-
pollinated. None escape the island. And those
that do, no one believes. Like: one
night Manoli heard his name
in a dream of nude acacias, and woke
to an eel licking his face. Its tongue flicked
his open eye and now
who can count the dead he knows?
When you approach in the fountain silence
of Sunday morning he lifts
his hand to hear the voices
traveling with you. If you ask, "How
does she want
her arrangement?" he scowls
like at a child interrupting grownups,
saying "Eva, your boy
forgets again. Yes, the dumb one. Do I tell
him?" before reciting with specificity the Latin
name of her favourite camellia,
yellow with a blood-red center. Cautiously,
because you're not to be
trusted with important things. Then
laughing at someone's joke
he carries on half in silence, and you tell
yourself, because you're

jealous, that he's insane. In the darkness
of the plane tree, two spies:
        swallow and nightingale.
A beetle hides its greenest leaf in a drain.
Before you leave he tugs your
        elbow and opens a bag
with an old tin of German
chocolates and a carton of cigarettes
        from the 1930s, whispering: "a magos
never tells." And you know
without checking it's your father's
        stash from the fake
hornet's nest in the bomb shelter. You take
a cigarette you don't smoke but keep
        in your coat pocket
till the filter wears out, and yellow flakes
of tobacco blend with lint.

Believers

mikro chorio, kako chorio
little village, evil village
—Greek proverb

Where do we begin to dig? The clouds. Not with prayer, but an adze. One day a stranger came to the village. What follows is a week of rain. Then a month. First it was a novelty: children paddled door to door by canoe. We played a cistern on the overturned piano. Then one day you discovered the translucence, and symptoms were everywhere. In fields of Latin names we didn't know leaves yellowed like codices. At night we cupped each other's ears to muffle the house's curling roots. Each face hid a flooded hive. Then one day we noticed the newcomer. How he drank no water but sat in a corner chewing the same limpid cabbage as us, growing sallow. Naturally it was him. At night the village is roused, the stranger mulched wide awake, staring at a hyacinth. With our eyes we begged forgive the spade and the hand that bore it through the skull. Things no one prayed for after: flowers, lost tools, time. Two weeks pass, then it stops. We congratulate ourselves on once again averting the flood. Story exonerates. We say clouds occasionally heal.

Burd

A man outlives three horses,
A stag outlives three men,
A raven outlives three stags
—*Proverbs of Munster*

I met a raven in her second life & brought
her silence to the water's edge,
strawflowers and shiny bits, she said: I'm
no a wean peeling pill bugs under greeny logs
wi a white streak in my hair. So
I brought her translations
of stag poems and for three weeks
she ghosted, always out with her friend
the blind monk in 1110 drafting *Book*
of the Dun Cow, till I stopped to consider
her needs, what she most coveted
in her darkest planets in the underlife
now youth is gone, and brought her
a slit thumb. And there she was:
fingers spread over water hum, a die-now
face on her face. Like wind stalking
the blood daub of a new cut flame: obey
and spool the labyrinth
wi his red thread of me or
kill him now? But
I too am wind when I want to.
Don't say I'm just a name
for everyone you've ever bled.
None of me fits in your mouth.

Minor Offerings

Before your body can scatter into crows again I'll take one in my hands and keep I don't know which part, maybe a left eye, and hold it until night falls and the rest of you has flown the haze line. It'll turn into a flame, a snake, a stone, a sprig of bloodroot. I'll hold it until it becomes a crow again and the sound of water uncurling the vertebrae of the ferns re-bodies the night. Behind the remembered moonlight a magnet tugs away a brightness until what is left resembles a dredged-up statue with half its face eaten. Like this bird waiting to shit in my hands. Who made out better? When I see you again you have a new eye, lighter. And I have a drawer full of dead crows.

Other Fountains

the blood of the bull
will run out fifty years from now

All parts of a bull are edible, even its shadow, which I am told is the best part. And in certain towns where people line up to purchase a thread of kidney or pearl of lymph from the slain bull, at times the flashing of knives goes on all night, the light separating blue from gauze, the smallest pixel of bull (which everyone admits, being muscular, tastes like a rubber shoelace) hung from the bell tower, around the necks of women, a vein of nacre still warm where ordinarily a locket would go—and the eligible bachelor, before leaping the terrace, bites a forelock of bristle and spits with two bloods the name of the bull, while in another frame children have covered the well and begin to dance, measuring with their steps in that darkening throat the voice of the bull, last to be eaten.

Your Bandura

I'm remembering your song with the red
star opening on a white horse's neck and wondering
        how in that room
of spilled cat litter and sheet music glued to
the hardwood floor you taught yourself
to play the accordion left-handed, next to the birdcages,
        the cigarette smoke
from the living room curling through the floorboards
all so you could manage the first twelve bars
of Bandura Waltz before switching the keys
        upright. And when
you did this live on Thursday night maybe one person
laughed and someone else in the audience,
the stranger you'd secretly rehearsed for,
        began to clap.
We were so broke I couldn't yet afford
to buy you a house in flames. I'm not sorry
I started in a half-tattered tailcoat stolen
        from the costume rack
in the old stage annex, with no symphony
but air and a dozen broke actors
waiting in the wings for the ungiven
        world to open. Though we
manage nothing quicker than decay.

Like a horse the village remembers
and at night when no one can see it
        it curls its neck
over your humming and pretends.

Instructions for the Cure

Wound a goat, but not mortally. Follow at a distance. You may cross: a drowned city, an earthly city. When you see the mountain, dress your scent in bloodstain. At no point let it read you above humus, hibiscus, exhaust. The dance is cruel but ancient. You'll know the goat by its six or sixty scars. This is why the mountain is black. Sometimes it takes hours, sometimes weeks: a quartz vein or jutty seam on craig face nursing the smell of lies. Take the forbidden root. Leave the other for the goat. You will know it by the taste of a previous life. A remaining cure—not because the goat and mountain are inextricably linked. Or because its geodes unfold venous birds. But once, to deter wolves, a shepherd grafted an antler and an agate to a goat's leg, its smell and pitch the mountain recalls from carrion and honeysuckle. Mountain-thing, blood-thing, still learning how to live with more than one soul: take this bitter herb. Remember none of it.

Fissure

Asleep, she imagines he is fishing on some horn-like reef of white water, his face so hardened from salt it's indistinguishable from the faces carved on his boat. It is a day he remembers, because he caught an eel with a red star over its eye, like the birthmark of his sister Evgenia. That night he dreamt he was reeling in the line half an hour when he noticed it was hair. He continued pulling until the hair gradually darkened and he realized there was blood on his hands. Returning home, he learned his wife had lost all her hair. Sometimes hands encounter a silence they do not immediately recognize, like the sound of a boat at night held by two ropes. With his thumb he climbs the red line to her scalp.

Gullwife

Hem-skirting mosses and tips
of wild garlic. Thirst sleeping

beside the mirror rocks. Bright
hair of lichen: sea-things taken

for body. In the ring-silence
of early morning she rose

from the bed where as nearly
children we planted more than

our shadows and less than a sea,
and followed with her hands

the rope fibers of a cormorant's
voice into a sky for none.

Dear Shipwreck

1.

A branch and a body float
by the same law.

The night brings back
ships, anchors,

posts green with oysters,
things lost long ago:

an emerald pin,
a frothy pearl

at the tip of a cufflink: luminescent,
like a votive candle

at the bottom of the bay—
spit olive pits and wine,

scented water, all of it
returned to the drawers, the tables,

the pockets of coats
suspended

on pegs touched
in the ship put back by waves,

the hole in the roof folded over
again, the planks salt-worn,

the balcony with its pots of herbs
replanted, and the going hand

of the fisherman who walked out
from the deck with two glasses

and tossing one into the sea
asked for nothing.

2. Victory at Sea

I do not believe in ghosts, but ghost ships
rise from the harbor
once a week, masts prodding

as they circle and cove
like lost dogs. The moon does not answer them.
The men wetting the foam

with piss at the docks
do not see them, or think they see
their own ships

night-fleshed and stout, dragging
one-by-one
the edible root of forgiveness

and feeling suddenly
wind enter
through gaps in the ribbing.

3. Capstan

Boat
  with its infections,
    an amalgam bit

of mercury and root
  cresting
    the chaffed wheat

of the wave.
  Boat
    in inflamed waters

glyphic,
  a dipped finger
    in a room of dark.

Chain-
  scrawled
    echolalia

of lo
  and rust on runnels
    of sand.

The lengthening
  rune
    of the rudder

unpronounceable,
  like the body's
    imperfect

sonar: all
  that is voyage
    untranslated.

4. Scuttle

I began it myself, from myself
assembled:

glinting light on the joists,

the sea-
architecture, a blue line

entering the vestibule

from the windows.
And when the sea consumed it

for the benefit

of salt, I sowed
hectares, barnacles, barnacles,

until my dwelling be

like a severed head on the water,
lolled.

But with even a milligram

of worm I'd build a proper field
with hooves and hedges, the lot—

windbreaks and bracken-

fed stems, planting corn
in a fish's eye. How we labored and

were made redundant

by pollinators
till they went scarce then it's back

again Jenny with the slender brushes

for pollinating each cucurbit
Adam spilt. O

be not gentle with the seed.

It isn't paper.
Sift it in a cup of vinegar and bee stings,

top dress it in ordinary

copper, like you'd wear
in a sandal to vex shipwrecks. Plant

        and be left

for bedlam
divers revelations.

5. The Progress

Tomorrow we clear bracken
for the orchard. I packed a
guidebook to know what to

do in the event of,
in case there should be
(even to speak

of it embarrasses) bloom,
in season or out, having
or not the white

I took for blanks
in an orchard when I stumbled
upon them as a boy and thought

I'd gone blind in one acre,
like the pastor said I would. But was
a living whiteness, fringed and

as I approached, maculate
with bees. Into calved
ice and glacier-tilled

substrate I worked a few cuttings,
apple mostly, and recalled
the soil's increase. The paper

hum of the leaf rot, our works
and days aerated
by earthworms from the Proterozoic

percolating the quartz
rim to bask in the glacier's
blade groove. It took

forever, and later I'm told,
sometime after us:
fruit.

III

Chimeras

My daughter says she is the Wolf Singer.
She plants the vertebrae of her enemies
like seeds. She's three.

I understand.
I too wear my antlers most of the time
now. It only hurts the first

hundred years. Sometimes she says:
I was here
before, I looked in the forest but

you were still a seed of you, not yet,
so I waited. In my daughter's
rock garden, today is water's birthday,

the moon is closing his eyes
for a haircut, and my secret crown keeps
getting caught on birds. Sing

with your first tongue
my daughter, we can't afford to be
human long.

Sonnet with Burn Leavings

Balancing on the reedy hem of the Tweed with a TV
antenna, prying up a brightness from flood pitch
imagining a brooch or tiara, green-tinseled but
inevitably coming up a ruminant's mandible circa
last winter, ungnawed but glamorous, like any
river beginning freed from a bottom, gone,
subtracted roiling bullet speed up then sunk
and up again, too quick to tell from foam.
In an afterlife I tend them: tibia, scapula, ilium,
os coxae, common as blackberries
used to be, washing up in cairn waters.
The newly brighted bane will slot in place
to a pulse of starlings. Watch the nearly animal
it makes resume its steady graze of static.

Found Letters in Translation

1.

My mastery of life extended only
to hollyhocks, my prized hundreds

coveting worms in their acres of gold.
It wasn't always easy, Pendré. Sometimes

I prayed for eighteen hours every day,
pocketing whelps from the cold, seed

droppings, and arranging them in the light
with a covetousness reserved for weevils,

and watched the satchels grow plump
and acoustic on the split wood, growing roots

in the sky for lack of earth. I saw them,
Pendré, their tall hairs filamenting

as they moved to one side, then the other,
collecting air. They seemed like wings

and soon I began to feel guilty
about keeping them in a glass cage

with all that breath in the world. It's true
what I said, Pendré, I let them go out

into the air, and they followed where I led.

2.

These writings are important, Pendré.
I had another daughter and I taught her

how to read, and now wherever
she goes there are not only irises

but their names, floating in her head
like another genus of flower.

I open her letters and petals
fall out. Pendré, did you know

she loves the tea. I make it every day
for her, sponging handfuls

of sage, marjoram, raspberry leaf,
veronica, Toulouse, spring gentian,

the open spaces, bonemeal, a marsh
cinquefoil uncurling in the water,

turning the bowl to sepia. Yesterday
I saw a ghost in the pantry

he said his name was Pendré too.
Sometimes I think I was born

at the end of my life and am living backwards.
This is how I explain my faulty memory.

Pendré, what if the day I met you
happened to be the day I died,

does that make us lifelong friends?
Is Pendré still your name, Pendré?

Pendré, the clouds are growing
the color of my daughter's eyes. I want

to protect her from the world, Pendré.
There are too many trees

for men to hide in, too many men
who have been to daughters what you

and I have been. Pendré, I haven't gone
to work in fifty years. Pendré,

do you think I can teach her how to live.

3.

The walls are clean today, Pendré.
I went for a walk in the rain

and when I came back there was
another man's coat on the hook.

I searched the house for him
and shouted at everyone.

Then I remembered it was my coat,
Pendré. This is what growing old is like.

I feel my handwriting getting worse
by the vowel. Did you know

the mugwort is growing?
I had a dream we were putting

on a play, one of yours, and half-
way through the third act the lights

went out and wouldn't come back on,
so we took off all our clothes

and spoke our lines in the nude.
Pendré, it was a ghastly sight

for all the moths and the rats
who could see us in the dark. Did

the cherries bloom sour one more time?
Are the hornets spinning houses

in the fallen crabapples? Is there still
enough light at night for reading

your memoirs in your lawn chair, Pendré.
Each day I pray to die but he says

there's one person still praying that
I live. Is it you, Pendré?

If it's you, will you stop.

What We Did When We Were Ghosts

I went missing for a time. There were sightings
in ordinary places, in the forest
near the turn by the trailhead
where others were reported to have vanished
wearing the color red. There's a
podcast: *Missing Person Joins Search for Self.*
It was raining. We found nothing.
Not the campsite or the path I took, the mountain
I was on, the language I spoke.
On the second day someone fell
into the ravine and was fished out
hypothermic and clutching a fistful
of women's hair. Around the fire
drinking condensed milk from tin cups,
one says: I've seen him in the branches,
his face was a beehive, his eyes two sick fruit.
Another says: in a dug-out canoe
with a black dog and red coins. Another:
went to school with him, sat beside him
in math, he didn't exist.
The next day it snowed. I couldn't find
my feet. We circled the ridge twice and noticed only
a naked woman dusting mushrooms.
Day three and some Boy Scouts showed up,
one found a moon rock. At night I see Middie
Rivers sitting by the fire next to his murderers.

In the morning a bunting of swans turn south and
we followed, waking up months later at the other end
of the trail, our rations eaten by bears and gluten
intolerant kids. Soon all of us are
missing. One group turned up in St.
Augustine, taken for cryptids in evacuated
houses. Another squatted near Boone,
wearing antlers to stave off barghests, early
frost. Somehow I'm found back
at Glastenbury Mountain.
My neighbors aren't serial killers
yet. The trailhead shines in October with
or without the first snow. And when
I enter the mountain sometimes I remember
to take it off again.

Leavings

Again I'm obsessing over the magentas. My grandfather
showed me to dress was to undress
the body in pigments—deer with prong end
raking lines in sand while its open half
pendulums, corrects when the gloved hand
tugs fuchsia from barbs along the spine. I didn't
know he was colorblind, and relied on codes
for divining green cabbage from red in
the scrawl of clay I'd plant a knife and watch
go to seed. In the afterlight blood
tastes like what passes for lager in 1960 when
he's teaching this to my father in
the ritual slant of a kerosene lamp behind
a shed even then on the verge of
collapse: a femur is a femur, it unlocks and draws
an N with the tibia and metatarsal when
the hind leg lifts at the first shot. Elbow-deep
in sang, paring edible from spoil,
red drawing a path of least. And because
like my father I'm eight and not yet
a pagan of the apparent, I wait for
a soul. Afterwards, headlights jaundice
trees, coolers hauled into the bed. Leavings
left for which creeping thing drags it away
overnight. The purple rivulet follows us
for miles, dirt to gravel, to
asphalt. Blood was always the road.

The Rabbit Hour

In the steam margins of cooling nettles
and three-cornered leek you called war

lettuces—early March foragings
from Ringwood—mushrooms

I was too nervous to harvest but you
didn't hesitate. Blind,

you knew them like bright daguerreotypes
in your mind, testing the hard rim

of a specimen of turkey tail with your
thumbnail, unsticking jelly ears from elder

bark. Later in the kitchen, your beard
and hair brightened by the fire musk

of cloveroot you'd retell: this time
of year assembled there some of us—

more than expected—witches
in a written spiral at Highcliffe-

on-Sea overlooking oblivion. Six months
after Dunkirk, we placed the brine

in our mouths and raised an almighty
thing—miraculous and humming,

a cone of power—stepping widder-
shins in a trilobite shape with a dusting

of poorly done Anglo-Saxon cants for vexing
wind. No sacrifice. Nothing to scatter

the Luftwaffe. But a needle-thought
to the Fuhrer's brain: you cannot cross

the sea. Did it work? How else
to explain the temporary respite from treble

and zrr-hiss: the rubble in the garden
without increase so the wisteria volunteers

could gain footing, the only invasive
for eleven weeks. Praise flowering

unasked for, and the willed interval
of a kitchen in silence at the first fringes

of twilight we called then the rabbit hour.

Providence

Provided water.
        Provided we remember
to cut fruit from its shadow.
Provided thunder
        & the machinations
of mycelium. The damp,
sieved night. Provided
the flotsam of wars,
        shells & ticking poppies,
the bank seeded with limbs
& canisters,
purpled birches radioactive.
Provided books
        for mulch, & fossilized pits
of plums
we spat as children
riding bikes in that world
still smelling of Technicolor.
Provided a parenthesis
        of spring
between bare & scald—we
could make for, possibly,
another
sixteen, seventeen
seasons: no
trial or providence, but

error in
diminishing hues
of carbon, no
beginning yet
to be seeded or faith
unnatural. Just
plant & forget
how
they said more &
we believed.

Passage

Girl and father
come to the edge
of a river, with no bridge,

no ferry, & something
enormous following
behind. The father

steps into the water
& becomes a boat.
She hesitates, then

steps onto planks that are
the color of his skin,
ropes like braids

of his hair, & the boat
is sent out across
the water like a word.

Like her mother who
in another dream walked
into the ocean with

her hands outstretched
to either shore until
she became a bridge—

thin & tapered like
a beeswax candle.
They crossed for

a mile over a darkness
they could not see, girl
& father, till they stood

on dry sand & the bridge
fell in silence like a branch
falling in snow. Now

she stands alone on
the opposite shore, &
the boat is only a boat.

Beginners

We filled in the pond with gravel and a cat skeleton
dug up from a corner of the yard and seeded
dahlias, red cabbage, grasses. I learn to plant
from a book I found in the wall of the toolshed
while adding insulation. Half the pages are missing.
Where it starts, a blank hydrangea like a ballet shoe
on an empty stage, deepening. I planted my hair
in the first acre to keep away rabbits and deer.
Someone ate it. I braided a fence, and a forgiveness
of ravens circled the blighted yews. I'm still learning
not to poison myself on the poke I took
for elder and propagated for its purple stain
on your lips. What do we know of the empty nests
we buried and sprinkled over with wood ash
for potassium? In this timeline we have possibly
two dozen years to accommodate a lifespan
of defeats. Please send cuttings.

Cuttings

In my death I heard the sound of water
like a moth stuck in a jar

& followed to where I woke in a field,
two sheep chewing

my handprint: fingers crimson & gorged
as rosehips. Alongside

irrevocable acts &
the lives of others so close

our own pain hums.
Because: how many

passing in the street or
on the train had a life from

which we chose
not to remain? Here

& there, inside
the hollow spiral rind of

my inner ear, where
a wasp queen spun her nest, I rose

adjacent to a life unrecognized & got on
with, noticing occasionally

in the burn & leaf smoke of my hair this
ripened buzzing.

Monster

mind says trap but
brightness is always
the thing you didn't taste

nets on the mountain wove
from a wren voice won't
touch my ankle

free from water I'll be
alone
with want & solve it

like a old-time remedy for
thirst: place
a stone on your tongue & suck.

Eat

go
no one will stop you
go on

a bird can be self-house-child
even an anchor
lifted a generation

to name the shore.
go where
word shape, island shape

the shock of shape in the orchard
where we meet
and have only this in common:

our grandmothers
knew how to fold
a chicken's breath

in under
surely under
fifteen seconds

to the next life without disturbing
the stains on their fingers.
expedient this memory smell

of week-old plum on the ground
wasp-spun and inoculated
in a night of dripping nets,

residue of salt which reddens
the edges of all my edges.
and because we share this

I know how to touch
your hair your shadow how to call
your most submerged and eardrum shattered

places
to surface and
what right have I

to be opened
completely.
the wave at the edge of us

waits. your plate of fruit
shines.
go on

raise the brightest skin
to your shadow's mouth.
I will be silence in my next life

the silence of an orchard's
root level
pressed between

water and dark, but for now
please
I want to hear you eat.